DADS SAY THE
DUMBEST THINGS!

DADS SAY THE DUMBEST THINGS!

A Collection of Fatherly Wit and Wisdom

**BRUCE LANSKY
& K.L. JONES**

Cover Illustration by Nina Cambron

⚏Meadowbrook Press

Distributed by Simon & Schuster
New York

Library of Congress Cataloging-in-Publication Data

Lansky, Bruce
Dads say the dumbest things: a collection of fatherly wit and wisdom/
Bruce Lansky and K.L. Jones.
    p.   cm.
    1. Fathers—Humor. 2. Fathers—Quotations. I. Jones, K.L. (Ken L.) II.
Title.
PN6231.F37L36   1989   818'.5402—dc20   89-29067

ISBN: 0-88166-131-7

Simon & Schuster Ordering #: 0-671-69613-0

Art Director: Sallie Baker
Production Manager: Pam Scheunemann

Published by Meadowbrook Press, 18318 Minnetonka Boulevard,
Deephaven, MN 55391.

BOOK TRADE DISTRIBUTION by Simon & Schuster, a division of Simon
and Schuster, Inc., 1230 Avenue of the Americas, New York, NY 10020.

00   15 14 13 12

Printed in the United States of America

CONTENTS

ACKNOWLEDGMENTS

We want to thank the following people for their creative contributions to *Dads Say the Dumbest Things:*

Bill Dodds
Tony Dierckins
Joe Delli Carpini
Mary McBride
Megan McLean
Sandy McCullough
Mitch Lansky
Jim Leba
Pam Scheunemann
David Wexler
Clara Jeffery

Special thanks are due to Bruce's dad, David, and Ken's dad, Robert Emlyn, without whom this book would never have been written.

INTRODUCTION

Dads really aren't as dumb as they seem.

It's just that something happens to dads when one kid has an "accident" and his diaper has to be changed at the same time that another kid falls and has an "owie" that has to be kissed . . . especially if all this happens while a big football game is on TV.

When dads are flustered, sometimes the only thing they can come up with is what their dads used to say. Even if what their dads used to say used to drive them crazy.

So that's why dads say:

- "When I say no, I mean no. Why? Because, that's why."

- "You're going to sit there until you eat your dinner. I don't care if you sit there all night."

- "If you don't stop crying, I'll give you something to cry about."

- "Can't you practice your drums quietly?"

- "I'm gonna stop the car, and I'm not gonna drive one inch until you stop fighting and shut up."

- "I'm spanking you because I love you. This hurts me a lot more than it hurts you."

- "I never had a car when I was your age, and I turned out just fine."

My dad used these lines on me. And as much as I hate to admit it, I used them on my kids too.

Ken Jones and I collected hundreds of "dadisms" into a book on the theory that when dads see them in print they'll realize how dumb many of their favorite expressions are. And if their kids let them know which ones drive them up the wall, dads will think twice before saying them.

I hope you'll read this book together with your family. You'll laugh a lot. I guarantee it. And you'll also learn what turns your kids off. If you're smart, you'll ask for their suggestions on what you should say instead. Then your kids won't think you're a whole lot dumber than you really are.

Bruce Lansky

P.S. There's one gem of fatherly advice I left out of this book, because it's not dumb. My father said it to me often, and if I'd listened to him, I would have saved myself a lot of needless worry.

"Do your best and leave the rest."

Thanks, Dad!

I'M THE BOSS

Father knows best.

Your mother might wear slacks, but I wear the pants in this family.

When I said it was "OK," I meant "maybe."

When I said "maybe," I meant "no."

And when I say "no," I mean "NO!"

I don't care what your mother said. We just won't tell her.

You're only five. If you want to live to see six, you'll do what I say.

When I say jump, you jump. All you have to worry about is how high.

I respect your opinion. Now shut up and listen.

Don't give me any of your lip, young lady.

What's so funny? Wipe that smile off your face.

You are grounded from now until the end of the world or when I say different. Whichever comes first.

Go to your room and don't come out until your beard touches the floor.

My house is a dictatorship, not a democracy, so you have no vote.

You have two choices. Either I'm right or you're wrong.

We'll do it the right way. My way.

I'll tell you why. Because. That's why.

I'm the boss and what I say goes.

God says I'm boss, that's who.

I'm your father, that's why.

Don't ask me, ask your mother.

A MAN'S HOME
IS HIS CASTLE

A man's home is his castle.

We bought this house with money I sweated blood for. . .when I borrowed it from your grandfather.

As long as you live in my house, you'll live by my rules.

I don't care what your friends do.

If all your friends jumped off the Brooklyn Bridge, would you jump too?

Don't leave your stuff all over the house for me to pick up. What do you think I am, your servant?

Your room looks like a trailer park after a tornado.

Will you be honoring us with your presence at dinner tonight?

Your mother cooks beef stew because I like beef stew.

You're going to sit there until you eat your dinner.

If you don't eat it you'll go to bed hungry.

I want to know who started it.

If you didn't do it, who did?

You want to run away? Go ahead. Just don't wire home for money.

Don't come back home and expect your mother to do your laundry.

From this day on, I have no son.

QUALITY TIME
WITH FATHER

Don't bother me when I'm watching my favorite show.

Not now.

Later.

Maybe tomorrow.

Never bother me when I'm watching football.

It's too nice outside to sit in front of the TV set.

Why don't you go outside and play?

On your way out, take out the garbage.

You can ride your bike in the street if you promise you won't get hit by a car.

Here's a buck. Go to the store and buy yourself an ice-cream cone.

You want something to do? I'll give you something to do.

It's about time you learned how to wash the car.

A little work never hurt anyone.

You're supposed to wash the car, not your sister.

What's wrong with you anyway?

You're not going to cry all day are you?

If you don't stop crying, I'll give you something to cry about.

Right now I'm going to read the paper.

I'm reading the funnies; why don't you read the editorials?

My father never helped me with my science projects.

When is your mother getting home anyway?

HIGH CULTURE

How come it never sounds like this when you play it?

Turn that stereo down.

You call that noise "music"?

Haven't you watched enough cartoons for one day?

If you watch too much TV, your brains will turn to mush.

Get out of the way. You make a better door than a window.

Don't sit so close to the TV; you'll ruin your eyes.

Read a book. Maybe you'll raise your IQ a few points.

What are you doing in the bathroom? You don't happen to have my *Playboy* in there, do you?

I don't subscribe to *Playboy* for the pictures. I only read the articles.

Everybody should know how to play a musical instrument.

You might hate the piano now, but when you're older you'll be glad I made you practice every day.

Can't you practice the drums quietly?

That doesn't sound like a violin; it sounds like a cat in heat.

Put some grease on your clarinet. Maybe it won't squeak so bad.

Sure your group can practice in the garage, but not while I'm home.

Don't worry. There'll just be your mother, myself, a few friends, and a hundred strangers in the audience.

You were the prettiest angel in the pageant.

No, I don't think anybody noticed that you forgot all your lines.

GAMES PEOPLE PLAY

OK, so you won. Big deal. This is a
dumb game anyway.

I don't care what the rule book says. We're playing by my rules.

If you want to win at Monopoly, be the banker.

When you're the banker in Monopoly, you can't keep all the money the other players give you.

I can't play with you now; I have work to do.

OK, you go hide and I'll count to a million.

Congratulations! That time it almost stayed out of the gutter.

If a golf ball is in the fairway, it ain't lost.

That would have been a good putt. But for a tee-shot it was lousy.

No, you can't take a point off your score for every tee you find.

If you lose one more golf ball, I'll lose you.

Don't throw horseshoes overhand. And never throw them at your sister.

You'll never beat your father in a million years.

I was almost drafted by the pros. Of course, I haven't played for a few years.

How come you always win when you keep score?

Want to go double-or-nothing?

We didn't buy a big-screen TV so you could play video games.

I know it's your game, but right now your uncle and I are playing.

LET'S GO
FOR A RIDE

Don't forget to buckle your seat belt.

I'm not going to start this car until you kids settle down and stop fighting.

How come when I told you to use the bathroom before we left home five minutes ago, you didn't have to go?

Quit horsing around. If you keep that up, I'll get in an accident.

No, we're not there yet.

We're not lost. I'm just not sure where we are.

Does anyone know where the map is?

Keep your hands to yourselves.

The truckers always know the best places to eat.

How can you be hungry? We ate five minutes ago.

You don't use the bathroom this often at home.

I'm gonna stop the car, and I'm not gonna drive one inch until you stop fighting and shut up.

Does anyone have change for the toll booth?

I told you before—we're not lost. Maybe they moved your aunt's house.

You can hold it in a little longer; we're almost there.

This looks like it, doesn't it?

I'm not going to let anybody out of this car until you kids stop fighting.

AN APPLE A DAY

You'll be the death of me yet.

Go to the dentist twice a year or you'll end up with teeth like mine.

False teeth are not fun.

Having your tonsils out doesn't hurt. Much.

Don't worry. It's only blood.

Either this thermometer is broken or the kid's dead.

If you don't behave, I'll send you to the doctor to get a shot.

If you shake it more than three times, you're playing with it.

Keep playing with it and you'll go blind.

Now where did I leave my glasses?

You don't know enough to come in out of the rain.

Hey, it's raining. Go out and shut the car windows.

If you've got a cold, stay away from the baby.

Funny, you don't look sick to me.

You throw up, you clean up.

There's no such thing as being allergic to spinach.

You never outgrow your need for milk—until you reach my age.

Coffee will stunt your growth.

Don't ever let me catch you smoking.

Smoking will stunt your growth.

If you weren't bigger than me, I'd take you over my knee and spank you.

Just because you've got a designated driver is no reason for you to be a designated drinker.

WHO'S GONNA FEED THE PET?

Sure he's a nice doggy. That's because I just fed him.
Before that he was eating my favorite hat.

What do you want a pet for? You've got a sister.

You can only get a dog if you promise to take care of it.

Today a kitty, tomorrow a cat, next week a litter.

If you don't empty the litterbox, I'm going to drown the cat.

Look. Fluffy left you a little present—right in the middle of the oriental rug.

I know you're supposed to change the paper in the bird's cage. But not until I've read it.

It's either you or the gerbils, and I'm leaning toward the gerbils.

When I said "feed the goldfish," I didn't mean "feed them to the cat."

Your goldfish ran away.

Kittens are cute; cats aren't.

If we name the kitten "Garfield," we'll get sued.

Don't tell your mother your pet snake escaped.

Lizards don't make good house pets.

Mary might have had a little lamb, but you can't.

They had to put Fido to sleep. I don't expect him to wake up in the near future.

MANNERS

Cute little devil—looks just like his old man.

No, you can't bring your Walkman to Aunt Minnie's funeral.

Big boys don't cry.

Your barn door's open.

Only girls play with dolls.

Young ladies don't climb trees.

If you fall out of that tree and break your leg, don't come running to me.

A lady would never trip a gentleman, especially not her brother.

Don't wipe off your aunt's kiss in front of her.

You should always say "please" and "thank you." That way you get more.

You shouldn't eat spaghetti with your fingers unless nobody is watching.

Spitting watermelon seeds is rude. Spitting them at your sister is suicidal.

Don't make Cousin Lenny laugh while he's drinking chocolate milk or it will come out his nose.

If you don't share it, I'm gonna take it back to the store.

Why do you always want to play with your sister's toys?

This is not a horses' stable; get your elbows off the table.

"Hey" is for horses.

Don't wipe your nose on your sleeve. Use some of that artwork you brought home from school.

Don't pick your nose—or anyone else's, for that matter.

DON'T YOU DARE

Don't you dare.

Whatever you're thinking, don't do it.

This is your last warning.

If I've told you once, I've told you a thousand times.

How many times do I have to tell you?

If you don't behave, I'll send you back to the pet shop where I bought you.

You better not let me hear about you fighting or I'll beat you black and blue.

If you play with fire, you'll get burned. And if you don't get burned, I'll spank you.

Don't do that if you want to sit down anytime soon.

And you better believe I mean it.

So you think you're tough, huh?

You and what army?

Over my dead body.

I'll call my lawyer and write you out of my will, and you won't get a penny.

Don't come crying to me.

If I hear one more scream out of your brother, you'll spend the rest of the afternoon in your room.

No, you can't go play with your sister in her room.

Straighten up and fly right.

Shape up or ship out.

You're grounded. You ain't goin' nowhere.

SPARE THE ROD

Where do you think you're going, young man?

Why don't you act your age? How old are you anyway?

If you act like a baby, I'll treat you like a baby.

You can't poke your brother in the eye just because the Three Stooges do it.

I'm gonna count to ten.

I don't know which of you did it, so the only fair thing to do is punish all of you.

Now you're really going to get it.

Just wait until I get my coat off.

I'm spanking you because I love you.

It hurts me a lot more than it hurts you.

OK, tell me why you did it, but I don't want to hear any excuses.

Don't give me that malarkey.

You wouldn't talk like that if your mother were here.

Silence is golden. So shut up.

If you say that again, I'll wash your mouth out with soap.

You have no respect for your elders.

Your grandfather spoils you. He sure didn't spoil me.

All I want is for you to know right from wrong. Lord knows it was hard enough getting you to know right from left.

STAY IN SCHOOL

You'd better be nice to your teacher
or she won't be nice to me.

So you think you're smart, do you?

You're not smart, you're a smart-ass.

I may not be a rocket scientist, but I am your father.

Sure I dropped out of high school, but there ain't nothing you can tell me that I don't already know.

"Ain't" ain't in the dictionary.

What did you do, sneeze and blow your brains out?

What's the matter? Don't you understand English good?

If you don't know something, don't be afraid to ask.

Don't ask so many dumb questions.

Algebra doesn't have to make sense.

If you don't learn geometry, you'll never be any good at pool.

"Voulez-vous couchez avec moi?" isn't French; it's smut.

You can't watch TV until you do your homework.

You can't watch TV while doing your homework, either.

What do you mean your teacher said you have to watch this TV show?

Finish high school or you'll wind up digging ditches like your brother.

I don't care if he makes $40,000 a year digging ditches.

I couldn't afford college so I went to the School of Hard Knocks. And I got my degree in Bumps and Bruises.

What are you going to do with a liberal arts degree?

No daughter of mine is going to be a professional wrestler.

HOLIDAYS

Just what I've always wanted.

Who wants to help trim the tree?

If you're naughty, Santa might not leave you any presents.

No Christmas gifts this year. Santa Claus was shut down by the Federal Trade Commission for a truth-in-advertising violation.

What do you mean you don't want to buy your sister a Christmas present?

Who wants to help me clean up all the needles and throw out the tree?

You don't celebrate on New Year's Day. You recover.

How come all I got was a Valentine card, and your mother got candy?

When you have a real job, you don't get to take Presidents' Day off.

What's so good about Good Friday?

The Easter Bunny wants you to find the eggs you missed last year.

Don't eat the chocolate bunny now, it'll spoil your dinner.

I'm just going to have a small piece.

Today is Mother's Day. Go bring her breakfast in bed. Then clean the kitchen.

This is Father's Day. I want to be left alone.

If it doesn't rain on the Fourth, we'll have a picnic and feed the ants.

I work hard all year. I get to take Labor Day off.

Don't eat any of your Halloween candy until I taste it—to make sure it's safe for you to eat.

Boy, am I stuffed. Thank God we only celebrate Thanksgiving once a year.

This is the best birthday I've ever had.

Now run outside and play. Mother and I want to take a little nap.

I'LL TAKE ROMANCE

I wasn't waiting up for you. I was just
reading the newspaper.

If you're waiting for Prince Charming to call, don't hold your breath.

Don't you know any normal boys?

There's lots of good fish in the sea—so start fishing.

How well do you know this guy who wants to take you to a drive-in movie?

He's not good enough for you.

You're not getting serious with him, are you?

Your mother did tell you about the birds and the bees, didn't she?

He's nice, but couldn't you find somebody with money?

I remember my prom night very well. I didn't go.

A date ends sometime before 1:00 in the morning.

I didn't go steady when I was in high school.

If he really loves you, he'll convert.

Nobody's worth changing your religion for.

You know, it's a lot cheaper to elope.

Remember: you only get married for the first time once.

You can't call off the wedding. I've already sent a down payment to the caterers.

How many toasters did you get?

Hey, for a first wedding it wasn't too bad.

WORK'S NO PICNIC

. . .and then when you become a millionaire, I'll retire
and you can support me.

I work hard to put food on the table—not to buy you designer jeans.

I've got to go to this convention in Bermuda. I just can't get out of it.

Working overtime is not like being sent to detention hall after school.

Being on strike is not the same as having the day off.

An assembly line is no picnic.

Jobs aren't supposed to be fun.

You can't retire after high school.

I don't know how much cowboys earn.

Someday you won't have your father to support you.

I would have been a doctor, but I couldn't stand the sight of blood.

I would have been a lawyer, but I don't like to read books.

59

Cooking is women's work.

Doing dishes is women's work.

Doing laundry is women's work.

Vacuuming is women's work.

Dusting is women's work.

There's nothing a man can't do if he tries.

WHEN I WAS
A KID. . .

I started shaving before they invented safety razors.
I almost lost an ear.

Y ou kids have it too easy nowadays.

When I was your age, I treated my father with respect.

My father would have killed me if I had pulled a stunt like that.

You think you have it tough? When I was a kid I had to work my way through elementary school.

I had a paper route, shined shoes, cut grass, and shoveled snow. Sometimes all in the same day.

When I was a kid, I knew the value of money. We never had any, but I knew its value.

No, I didn't know Abe Lincoln when I was a kid.

No, they haven't invented any new numbers since I was a kid.

A slide rule was sort of like a calculator without batteries.

Latin was a dead language even when I was a kid.

What do you mean, you never heard of *Sputnik?*

At least you don't have to worry about being drafted.

I always got good grades.

I was very popular in high school even if your mother doesn't remember me.

Your mother was a saint, but she's changed a lot since then.

THE VALUE
OF A BUCK

Easy come, easy go.

Whando you need an allowance for?

When I was your age I had to work for my allowance.

Didn't we give you lunch money last week?

You're only six. You don't need a credit card.

No toy is worth $29.95.

If you want it, you pay for it.

Instead of sitting around like a bump on a log, you could be outside mowing the lawn.

You think mowing the lawn is hard work? I had to bring in the fall harvest with a pitchfork.

All play and no work makes Jack a lazy bum.

Early to bed, early to rise, work like a dog, and advertise.

Nothing is going to be handed to you on a silver platter, except maybe a dead duck.

There's no such thing as a free lunch, except at the Salvation Army—and they make you march around the block beating a drum.

Money isn't everything, but it sure beats living on food stamps.

Money doesn't grow on trees. If it did, everyone would want to be a forest ranger.

Interest is money you pay the bank because you didn't have enough money.

Why don't you get a job, earn some money, and pay rent—like me.

I never had a car when I was your age and I turned out just fine.

THE MEANING
OF LIFE

Life doesn't always go according to plan.
Ever heard of "Murphy's Law"?

Life is not a bowl of cherries; it's more like a box of rocks.

Who said life is supposed to be fair?

Do unto others before they do unto you.

Life is what you make of it.

Life is what they make out of you.

Today isn't the first day of the rest of your life. It's Tuesday.

The early bird gets the worm—but the early worm gets eaten.

The best things in life cost more than we can afford.

Some clouds have silver linings, and some clouds have brown linings.

You're only young once, and then you get senile.

Someday you'll understand—if you live long enough.

Life is like a football game. Eventually you run out of time.

Life is tough, and then you die.

FREE ADVICE

Stay away from squirrels; they collect nuts.

D on't do anything I wouldn't do.

Do what I say, not what I do.

Make something of yourself. Don't be a bum like your Uncle Herb.

If you don't learn from your mistakes, somebody else will.

Never play cards with a man named "Doc," and never go to a doctor you play cards with.

It's better to be safe than sorry, but it's better to be sorry than dead.

Keep your nose to the grindstone, your eye on the ball, and the rest of your face will take care of itself.

As long as you do your best, nobody should complain. They will. But they shouldn't.

Don't cry over spilled milk. Let the cat lick it up.

If you can't do it right, don't bother doing it at all.

If you can't do it right, make sure you don't get caught.

You won't always have your brother to blame it on.

God helps those who help themselves.

What do you mean you won't need God's help if you help yourself?

You can do anything you set your mind to.

You can't always get what you want.

Don't expect your problems to go away by themselves.

You can't stay locked in that closet forever.

WE THE PEOPLE

The cost of the White House has gone up since the
Kennedys bought it.

You have a right to your own opinion, but you'd better change it.

"Born in the USA" is not the national anthem.

This is a democracy, and that's why you'll believe what I tell you to believe.

There ought to be a law against that.

Nobody can tell me what to do. This is America.

Free speech doesn't mean you can use words like that.

Cheating on your income tax is the American way.

In America, anyone can grow up to be president, and sometimes they do.

Nobody remembers vice presidents.

Voting is a sacred responsibility for every citizen in a democratic society.

I didn't vote because it was only a primary.

That's not a shower. It's a polling booth.

I'm voting for her because she's the best man for the office.

All politicians lie. That's how they get elected.

OH, MY GOD!

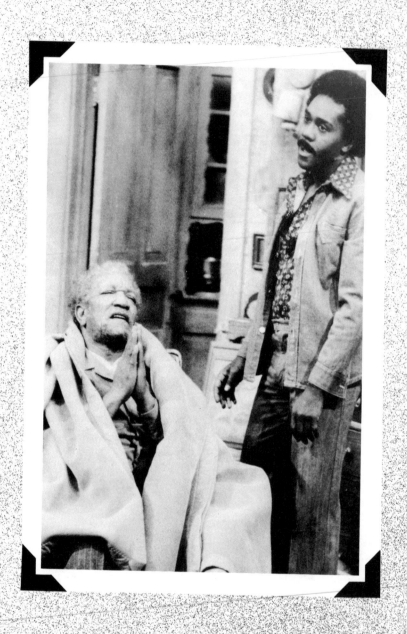

You'd better say your prayers and hope
to hell God hears them.

You can't be a nun. You're a boy.

Ministers don't have to make sense.

Pay attention to the sermon.

What do you mean, I was snoring?

Good people go to heaven, and bad people go to hell. Guess where you're heading.

Don't laugh in church or you'll burn in hell.

Heaven is air conditioned. Hell isn't.

You put money in the basket. You don't take money out.

That's not a cookie; it's a communion wafer and you can't bring it home for the dog.

The priest doesn't have to read you your rights before he hears your confession.

All God wants is for you to do what I tell you to do.

If you say your prayers every night, God will watch over you.

God is always watching you.

God is everywhere.

God knows everything about you.

God is not a snoop.

THE EMPTY NEST

Boy is he cute. He looks just like me.

So now you have a good job, drive a sports car, and rent a fancy apartment. You want to borrow a couple of bucks?

Seriously, is everything OK?

You know you can always move back home.

Don't be a stranger.

Your mother tried to call you last night. Where were you?

How come you never call?

You should stop by some time.

Your mother worries.

You've lost weight.

Isn't your wife feeding you?

When are we gonna get a grandchild?

What do you mean, a baby would interfere with her career?

You were never that cute.

I guess the brains skipped a generation.

Have more than one kid.

Your mother and I would like to take the kids to Disney World.

What do you mean, I'm spoiling your kids?

FAVORITE
BEDTIME STORIES

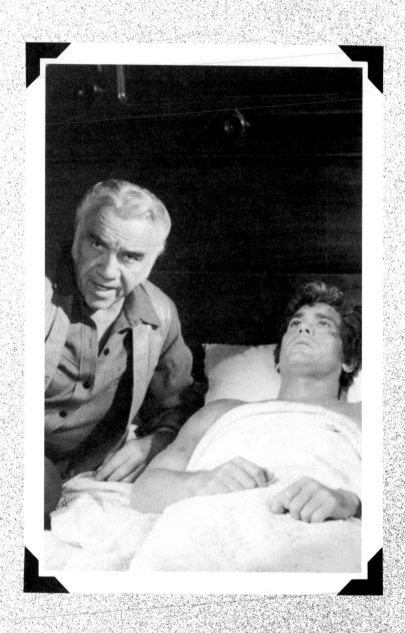

Once upon a time there were three bears.

Once upon a time there were three bears. But a hunter shot them. And they all lived happily ever after—except for the three bears.

I don't know if Little Red Riding Hood was related to Robin Hood.

Once upon a time was probably before I was born.

Humpty Dumpty sat on a wall. Humpty Dumpty had a great fall. All the king's horses and all the king's men had scrambled eggs for breakfast.

Rudolph had a bad cold—that's why his nose was so red.

I don't think Pinnochio met Jonah in the whale.

Once upon a time there was a boy named Jack who traded a cow for some beans and grew a beanstalk that was so big a giant almost ate him. So he cut down the beanstalk. And they all lived happily ever after—except for the giant.

Cinderella might not have married the prince if the footman had used a shoehorn.

When you wish upon a star, make sure it's not a UFO.

Once upon a time there were seven dwarfs: Dopey, Sleepy, Bashful, Doc, Larry, Curly, and Moe. So, after Snow White ate the poisoned apple, she fell asleep until the prince came and kissed her. Then they got married and lived happily ever after because she never invited her stepmother to come and visit.

Fairy tales don't come true. Except in books.

I'm not gonna tell you another story.

OK, one last story. Once upon a time, something happened. Then everybody lived happily ever after. Now go to sleep.

DUMB THINGS
MY DAD SAID

Paste your
father's
picture here.

This space is for writing down your dad's favorite
expressions. (Not too bright, are they?) We've
probably listed many of your father's favorites in the
preceeding pages. But part of the fun of being a dad
is coming up with your own lulus. So if you've got
some great "dadisms" that aren't in this book,
please send them to: Dads' Sayings, Meadowbrook
Press, 18318 Minnetonka Blvd., Deephaven, MN
55391. If we use them in a subsequent edition, we'll
give you a credit line.

_____

_____

_____

_____

_____

_____

_____

_____

_____

_____

DUMB THINGS MY DAD SAID

TV DADS COUCH POTATO QUIZ

Test your knowledge of the "wit and wisdom" of TV dads. Try to match the TV dad with his quote. The correct answers are listed on the next page. A perfect score means you're a perfect couch potato.

1. Archie
"All in the Family"

2. Jed Clampett
"Beverly Hillbillies"

3. Fred Flintstone
"The Flintstones"

4. Fred Sanford
"Sanford and Son"

5. Ward Cleaver
"Leave it to Beaver"

6. Steve Keaton
"Family Ties"

7. Clifford Huxtable
"The Cosby Show"

8. Howard Cunningham
"Happy Days"

9. Ricky Ricardo
"I Love Lucy"

10. George Jetson
"The Jetsons"

11. Pappy Maverick
"Maverick"

12. Herman Munster
"The Munsters"

13. Gomez Adams
"The Addams Family"

14. Al Bundy
"Married . . . with Children"

a. "Whee Doggies."

b. "Remember, it's better to give than to get five across the lips."

c. "Maybe our baby was switched with one of the Rockefellers.'"

d. "I'm getting frisky, Marion."

e. "Yuse got some 'splaining to do."

f. "Darn, Darn, Darn, Darn, Darn, Darn!"

g. "Everybody in high school said that nobody was dumb enough to marry the big redhead."

h. "Shut up, you!"

i. "Help, help—somebody do something."

j. "I hope you learned your lesson."

k. "I brought you into this world; I can take you out."

l. "Jane! Stop this crazy thing!"

m. "Stay clear of weddings because one of them is likely to be your own."

n. "Tish, I love it when you speak French."

Answers on next page.

ANSWERS

1. h	8. d
2. a	9. e
3. i	10. l
4. b	11. m
5. j	12. f
6. c	13. n
7. k	14. g

Moms Say The Funniest Things!
by Bruce Lansky

Bruce Lansky has collected all the greatest lines that moms have ever used to deal with "emergencies" such as getting the kids out of bed, cleaned, dressed, to school, to the dinner table, undressed, and back to bed. This book includes such all-time winners as: "Put on clean underwear—you never know when you'll be in an accident;" and "If God had wanted you to fool around, He would have written the Ten Suggestions." This book is a fun gift for mom.

Order # 4280

Golf: It's Just a Game
selected by Bruce Lansky

Bruce Lansky has hit a hole-in-one with this collection of funny golf quotes from such devotees of the game as Lee Trevino, Gerald Ford, Bob Hope, and many more. The book is illustrated with some of the cleverest cartoons ever to appear in *Golf Digest* and *Playboy*.

Order # 4035

Kids Pick the Funniest Poems
selected by Bruce Lansky

Three hundred elementary-school kids say that this book contains the funniest poems for kids—because they picked them! Not surprisingly, they chose many of the funniest poems ever written by such favorites as Shel Silverstein, Jack Prelutsky, Jeff Moss, and Judith Viorst. This book is guaranteed to please children ages 6–12!

Order # 2410

Familiarity Breeds Children
selected by Bruce Lansky

Originally published as *The Funny Side of Parenthood*, this collection of the cleverest and most outrageous quotes and cartoons about raising children has been repackaged to make it an even more appealing gift for parents, new and old. Includes the best of yesterday's and today's humorists: Roseanne, Erma Bombeck, Bill Cosby, Dave Barry, Mark Twain, Fran Lebowitz, and more.
Order # 4015

Age Happens
selected by Bruce Lansky

The perfect gift for anyone who has celebrated their 39th birthday more than once! A compilation of the funniest quotes and cartoons about growing older by the most insightful wits of all time, including Ellen DeGeneres, Robert Frost, Garrison Keillor, Bill Cosby, Ashleigh Brilliant, Leo Durocher, and many more! This book includes 15 black-and-white cartoons by some of *The New Yorker's* most popular cartoonists.
Order # 4025

For Better And For Worse
selected by Bruce Lansky

This entertaining collection of quotes and cartoons about marriage is an ideal gift for wedding showers, bachelor/bachelorette parties, anniversaries, and birthdays. Roseanne, Jerry Seinfeld, Rita Rudner, Bill Cosby, Richard Lewis, and many other notables are quoted at their hilarious best!
Order # 4000

**Look for Meadowbrook Press books where you buy books.
You may also order books by using the form printed below**

Order Form

Qty.	Title	Author	Order #	Price (U.S. $)	Total
	Age Happens	Lansky, B.	4025	$7.00	
	Are You Over the Hill?	Dodds, B.	4265	$7.00	
	Best Baby Shower Book	Cooke, C.	1239	$7.00	
	Best Party Book	Warner, P.	6089	$8.00	
	Best Wedding Shower	Cooke, C.	6059	$7.00	
	Dads Say the Dumbest Things!	Lansky/Jones	4220	$6.00	
	Familiarity Breeds Children	Lansky, B.	4015	$7.00	
	For Better And For Worse	Lansky, B.	4000	$7.00	
	Games People Play	Warner, P.	6093	$8.00	
	Golf: It's Just a Game!	Lansky, B.	4035	$7.00	
	Grandma Knows Best	McBride, M.	4009	$7.00	
	How to Line Up Your Fourth Putt	Rusher, B.	4075	$7.00	
	Italian without Words	Cangelosi/Carpini	5100	$6.00	
	Lovesick	Lansky, B.	4045	$7.00	
	Moms Say the Funniest Things!	Lansky, B.	4280	$6.00	
	Over-the-Hill Party Game Book	Cooke, C.	6062	$3.95	
	Pick A Party	Sachs, P.	6085	$9.00	
	What's So Funny about Getting Old?	Noland/Fischer	4205	$7.00	
			Subtotal		
			Shipping & Handling		
		MN residents add 6.5% sales tax			
			Total		

YES, please send me the books indicated above. Add $2.00 shipping and handling for the first book with a retail price up to $9.99, or $3.00 for the first book with a retail price over $9.99. Add $1.00 shipping and handling for each additional book. All orders must be prepaid. Most orders are shipped within two days by U.S. Mail (7–9 delivery days). Rush shipping is available for an extra charge. Overseas postage will be billed.
Quantity discounts available upon request.

Name _____

Address _____

City _____State _____ Zip _____

Telephone (_____) _____

Payment via:

☐ Check or money order payable to Meadowbrook (No cash or COD's please)

☐ Visa (for orders over $10.00 only)   ☐ MasterCard (for orders over $10.00 only)

Account # _____

Signature _____ Exp. Date_____

You may also phone or fax us with a credit card order.

A *FREE* Meadowbrook catalog is available upon request.

Mail to: Meadowbrook Press, 5451 Smetana Drive, Minnetonka, MN 55343
Phone 952-930-1100   Toll-Free 800-338-2232   Fax 952-930-1940
For more information (and fun) visit our website: www.meadowbrookpress.com.